AF414148

Moments on the Journey

Poems by Aram Kabodian

Moments on the Journey
By Aram Kabodian

"Dear Southern Nevada" originally shared
at nvartscouncil.org/nevadan-to-nevadan-gallery/

"Lisa" originally published in
Voices of Michigan: an anthology of Michigan authors, Vol. 3,
Mackinac Jane Publishing Company, 2001

Cover photos by Aram Kabodian

Contents

Dedicated to Bob Rentschler

"I know the mirror
will arrest me one day soon
        maybe tomorrow
but all is grace today."

From Bob's poem, "The Gift"

With You

I Steer Towards You

I'd rather be early than late, so I am
Prefer the shade to the sun, when I can
Whiskey at night
Water's all right with me
You see…

(chorus)
Goin' with the flow is my usual direction
But if you need me, I steer towards you
And thinkin' of my self comes first most days
But if you need me, I steer towards you

I can't be my best self unless
I first put the oxygen mask on me
Tell me if you need my ears and my eyes
And you have them as long as you need

(chorus)
Life's a bitch sometimes for us all
You might notice I disappear some
Time alone feeds me and I'll be back
I'll be singin' my usual song

(chorus)
Whiskey at night
Water's all right with me
And you are all right with me
You are all right with me

Lisa

I used to write her love notes,
often.

      She was a cheerleader and snow queen,
        and second chair flute
           (played melody...
              happy notes...)

     I was
      nobody really,
        eighth chair clarinet
          (played background...
            low, whole notes)

She was kind about it,
seemed to read them.
Wrote back once
or twice.

      Short notes of recognition
        (locks off a goddess, left-overs,
         charity)
I kept them in my pocket
for weeks.
They'd get so the ink would blur
from the sweat
in the creases of my pants.
I didn't care --- I knew the words

    by heart...she called me
    "sweet," "a nice guy," "a good friend."

I wonder if she ever told
anyone.
    Was I a secret
        or
    the laughing stock of the girls' locker room
    and the flute section?
        (don't fool yourself,
        you were a big-time secret...
        embarrassing, curious, weird)

Last I heard,
she was teaching English in   Minnesota.

I taught English in some of the same
rooms that I gave her notes in
almost   twenty   years   earlier.

I hadn't thought of her for years
and then
I intercepted a note
passing among my 7th graders.
Sealed very well --- taped, stapled.

"I love you, love you, love you Lisa.
                         --- Jay."

The class wanted me to read it
aloud.

      It was like she walked through
      the door and looked me straight
      in the eye.

I put it in my pocket.

At the end of the hour,

I gave it to Lisa

        one more time.

What She Said

"You deserve to be happy"

My friend's words
woke me
empowered me
reminded me

of that simple truth

freed me, really

though it took me
several years
to work my way out

to make
the excruciating choice
to live
my life
instead of what others
constrained me in

I was   relatively   happy
Things were   okay

Her words shook me
into an alternate world
enlightened my mind

to want more than okay
to not have to work at
happy
so hard

Happy turns out to be
options
Happy turns out to be
making my own decisions

Happy
is as simple as
not making the bed

or on a whim
to make the fucking bed
but not perfectly

Happy will be a long road
but it's my road
now

What If?

My therapist prods me
to unearth forgotten
horrific moments
from my early years.

What need did I have
that went unmet?

What unrealistic expectation
was I asked to fulfill?

"Picture yourself
in that space —
What does it smell like?
What is happening
or what is not happening
that you wanted
to happen?"

He hopes to help me
explain certain behaviors
I exhibit and thoughts
I entertain. He's looking
for the dark answers.

And it occurs to me…

What if
I had a fucking fabulous

childhood?

Every frickin' need met
realistic expectations
here, there, and everywhere
every frickin' day
of my hilariously
awesome elementary,
middle,
and high
years?!

What if
my issues are the
result of some other
phenomenon?
        fate
        bad luck
        not enough faith or too much
        chance
        a toxic blend of high-fructose
                corn syrup and
                Calculus
        not enough ice cream

What if Freud was wrong
and I can't blame
my mother, father, id, ego, super
ego, instincts, my doctor, or even
Carl Sagan?

It's possible.

There may be nothing dark
to remember.
All that prodding
just an expensive ruse,
a ridiculous waste of time,
a futile Etch-a-Sketch charade,
fleeting artistic scenarios.

I for one
am not counting out anything.
Except the negativity…
I am excluding the negativity.
It loses. I say so.

Four a.m.

Four a.m. is an old friend
Who's been there
For me at some tough times.
We see each other
And take up where we left off.

Four a.m. knows I like to write,
Then read,
To get back to sleep.
Four a.m. is gender non-specific,
Like God,
And can tell when I have something
On my mind that
I am hesitant to discuss.

Four a.m. gives me that look
And I get out my journal
And get writing.

When we met, I was in a hurry
To get back to sleep,
Ignoring the offer of friendship.
Over the years, I have welcomed
Their embrace.

Four a.m. understands me
In ways no one else does.
Listens with extreme patience,
Let's me be my authentic self.

I wonder
Do others know Four a.m.
As intimately I do?
I don't wonder enough to bring
Four a.m. up in polite conversation –
That would break our pact,
Almost feel like cheating.

And Four a.m. knows when we need
To step away for awhile.
They tap me on the shoulder
And say
"Go back to sleep."

Too Personal

I want to write a poem
about sexual relations
at sixty four

I want to write a poem
about having tough,
important conversations
about sex and sexual identity
with an adult son

I want to write a poem
about the pain of
a daughter not talking
to a father for over a year
because she's not ready for
the realities and intricacies
of her parents' divorce and/or
she judges her father's behavior
as sexist

I want to write a poem
about the whole of the grief
of divorce, including the
hell it is having any relationship
with your ex

I want to write a poem
about how retiring from

teaching is another kind
of grief; maybe like having
a phantom limb

I want to write
too many poems
that I don't really
want you to read

So I won't write them

But this poem shared
some of those feelings
and that's all you get

We are Each Other's Butterflies

For Delvar and Bonnie
And for Linda

Each radiating individual beauty
Meant to fly around the other
Attracted and at home
In the other's presence
Both having been transformed
For these moments and
In these moments —
This short, beautiful journey
We fly together

(Potential) Farewell Party

The timing would be tricky.

When to pull together
All the (un)interested parties —

teachers from my team,
card-playing friends,
Church choir members,
And other fans of my ex-wife

As well as ex-brothers-in-law
And ex-sisters-in-law
Ex-father-in-law
A few ex-nieces
        And their families

The location would be easier

An out-of-the-way hall
At least an hour's drive
from all of them —
make it inconvenient
As hell
But make it mandatory —
"Your therapist requires the
(dis)pleasure of your company."

But the timing

Would be a bitch

Later in the process
I would think

The day the divorce
Is final seems
Appropriate,
Though often
Hard to predict
In advance
        And could be
        Traumatic
For the adult children
Should they feel the need
To attend

And afterwards,
Things get so messy
With decisions whether
Or not
To un-friend me
Block my calls
Etcetera

The Farewell Party
For all-those-who-plan-
To-cut-me-
Out-of-their-lives

Seems like it would be
A healthy tradition

To begin though

Give us all a chance
To say what's on our minds.
A public airing of
Grievances —
Major and minor
Complaints.

And then we would
Be done with it

Clarity and closure
And possibly fewer
Passive-aggressive dreams
To sort out
Down the road.

You'll thank me someday.

Amazing Dad

Hey, Dad
Guess what I did today?
I put gas in my car
And paid for it with my
phone
Amazing, huh?!

And cars can park by themselves
Some can drive themselves…
Though not very well.

And remember your indoor putt putt idea?
That's happening now,
Often combined with an arcade, laser tag,
Food, and even gambling sometimes.

Even more amazing is that our country
Twice elected a self-serving President
Who has alienated us from our allies.
It's not going so well.

You'd be amazed at this crazy wonderful
World, Dad.
And you were quite amazing yourself.

I see you behind the camera,
Framing us.
Sometimes, you'd run to be in the movie.
I didn't realize until years later

That taking super 8 movies in the 60s
Was a big deal.
Family documentarian.

I hear you on the phone
From when I would call you
For advice on fixing things
Around the house.
You were always generous
With ideas for jimmy rigging
A screen door,
An exhaust pipe on a car,
Ceiling fans,
Whatever wasn't working.
Problem-solver extraordinaire.

I sensed your awe at the world.
So much that I quote your
"What a system!" phrase often.
You seemed genuinely
Wonderstruck at the way the world ran.
And I share that awe.
Reverent observer.

I remember you helping many
A stranded motorist,
Which took guts and confidence –
Though it always just seemed
Like the right thing to do to you.
A Boy Scout's boy scout.

I'm not saying you were perfect
And for that too, I thank you.
"We're all doing the best we can"
You'd say,
Sometimes I'm not so sure,
But I like to think you're right.

None of us feel like we had enough
Time with you, Dad.
I still hear your laugh
And can see you slap your knee
With delight.

Your 100th birthday would have been
Amazing
But the 79 you gave us
Were a gift –
YOU, were a gift, Dad.
Nearly a perfect 300 game, in bowling lingo.

Observing

Bewildered

The man on the moon
is late for work

He can't find his keys
(or his fingers or his legs)

He seems bewildered
by his whole predicament

Forgetting, I guess,
his disembodied state

Moving ever so slowly
in his hunt for his keys

His floating could make
you think he didn't really

Want to go to work, after all

Dear Grandma

The island is just like you said it was. Horses greeted our ship
at the dock. They pulled the carriage we rode up to the fort. As I listened
to the driver, I thought about you. when you came here as a child
on that cruise ship. This postcard reminded me of the smoke from the top
of your cruise ship. I saw the statue of Pere Marquette in the park. Pigeons
still like the view from on top of his head. And we went through Fort Mackinac
and heard the soldiers fire their muskets. I liked looking out from the fort and
seeing our ship. I could even see the deck chair that I napped in.
On the carriage ride back, I sat up in front so I could see the horses'
powerful movements. How they practically know where to go without the driver.
And I heard them, Grandma. Heard their heavy breathing and felt their majesty,
like you said. And I saw kids riding bikes down Main Street just like you did.
It hasn't changed, Grandma. I wanted you to know, it hasn't changed.

Love, Anthony

Pausing

Flying
seems like a fast way
to get across
great distances

When I am in a plane,
though,
looking out the window
we appear to be
moving fairly slowly

On the one hand,
I know we are covering
miles quickly — I can see
the football fields and
shopping malls pass by
in seconds — but I experience
our movement at snail speed

The plane moves so slowly
that, at times,
we seem to pause in mid-air

Usually, the pausing leads to
a bank left or right
or some other change
but for a moment
the plane appears to practically
stop

And I wonder why we don't fall —
a weight of over 180,000 pounds
stopping in mid-air —
could the reason have something
to do with God reminding us
to think before we act?
God allows gravity's power
to be suspended thousands of times
a day
for that single purpose:
"Hey you…pause and consider
what you're doing before you
change course," God says
quietly

If we'd only listen

This Moment

> Long, thin palm leaves
> Sway in the warm breeze –
> Casual confidence of youth

this precious moment
of blessed silence

helping me focus
on my breath

every moment
will never happen again,
    glorious, Godly sunrise
    as well as the grey one

gratitude in this moment
so sacred
so alive
so present

Retirement Benefits

    Tier 1

On those days
You don't feel like
doing anything,
      you don't do anything

Naps!
      spontaneous, random, plentiful

Lower tax bracket

The library is your second home,
Employees call you by your first name
and if you forget your coffee mug,
it's at the front desk the next day

More opportunities to exercise
should you feel inclined or
have a doctor insist upon it

Snacking is a blessing and a challenge

Puzzles and games pass the time

Read that book you've been
meaning to read
Write the great American novel
(or a poem about retirement)

See the parents, children, grandchildren,
nephews, nieces…more…and just enough

Learn a new skill
Start a new hobby
Or perfect old ones

Pickleball!

Attend a day game of your favorite baseball team

Silliness becomes a regular option

Stop wearing a watch

Tier 2

Empty your bladder completely
instead of rushing

Intimacy opportunities increase

Protest without fear you'll lose your job

One could volunteer and/or work
When and if one feels the call,
Mentor or tutor even if needed

Travel until the money runs out

Thank God for every day

Choosing Discomfort and Gratitude

I.

Twenty of us crawled in
To the small tent-like space
Of bent willow branches
Covered by many blankets.

We each found a spot
To sit on the ground
In the darkness of
The sweat lodge.

As the door closed
We witnessed
Can't-see-our-hands-
In-front-of-our-faces blackness.

II.

I noticed
The voice first.
A soaring native song
Of beauty,
Of instruction,
Of reassurance.

The hiss of water on hot rocks
Caught my attention;

My face, arms, legs
Began sweating profusely.

The moist air was thick
Entering my lungs —
Just as I started to panic
        I remembered
To place my face on the ground
To find the coolness.

My uncomfortableness
Soon faded. I relaxed
And sat up again.

Next, we each spoke,
Recalling great spirits.
Thanking each one
For the gifts they had given
For the joy and laughter
For life lessons taught.

III.

After a time mixed with song
And a deep connection with others
And waves of heated, humid air
And voices familiar and foreign,
Speaking of people familiar and foreign
And my inability to stretch
And the discomfort of it all
Just starting to feel at home with the uncertainty,

I was suddenly out
In the bright light
Able to breathe a welcome, pure air
And stretch
And see
Anew.

Scouting

Haven't we all been there?

It's your first time
You have a plan
     you're eager to be a part of
     this event

Then the wind changes
     and the next thing
     you know
You have a flag in your face
Wondering why
You're doing this at all,
Hoping no one is watching

The scout on the right, though,
Seems to be taking it all in stride
        left hand behind his back,
        standing at attention and waiting
        for the morning cannon to fire
        and the command to raise

I wonder why he is standing on the grass
He's a scout — cheerful, obedient, reverent —
Is he also a rebel
Or just a bit different?

There is a blank space in the photo
And that is where I see myself,
Flag in my face
Wrestling with the rope
Maybe even looking out
From behind my flag
At the Scout Barracks
At my scout buddies
At this guy taking the photo

Wanting to be him

Excerpts from Life

"Sometimes my grief feels
as though I've been left alone
in a room with no doors."

      My sister's husband died
      unexpectedly
      during surgery;
      she's been wandering
      around her life for
      almost several years
      looking for a door.

"The instant
there is no chance of death
is the moment of death."

      I am sitting on a Boeing 737
      in a middle seat
      amid over two hundred
      masked passengers;
      I decide to munch
      on my complimentary pretzels.

"All safety is an illusion,
but maybe it doesn't
feel that way
if your position
in society has not
only given you power
but also protected you

from the experience of being,
and of feeling,
powerless."

> I become aware
> of my privilege
> at age 45 —
> while recounting a story
> to a Black friend —
> of when I wasn't arrested
> after doing something stupid
> at the age of 19.

"Stay hungry. Stay foolish.
Never let go of your appetite
to go after new ideas,
new experiences,
and new adventures."

> In the midst of administrative
> worries about test scores,
> I propose a buddy program
> between our middle schoolers
> and the first graders
> across the street
> for literary and social bonding
> and fun.

Excerpts from…

Crying in H Mart: A Memoir
by Michelle Zauner

"Irreconcilable Dissonance"
by Brian Doyle in *One Long River of Song*

"On White Violence, Black Survival, and Learning to Shoot"
quoting James Baldwin
by Kim McLarin in the *Sun Magazine*

back cover of the 1974 *Whole Earth Catalog*
Steve Jobs

My Bad

I had this one student,
Jenny —
she was enthralled by
dramatic irony —
        when we know something
        in a book or movie
        that the characters don't know

She would always notice it first —
        early in Hemingway's
        "A Day's Wait," her hand
        would shoot up
"The boys thinks he's going to die,
but we know he just has a fever"

Jenny now writes
for the Hallmark Channel
and has worked dramatic
irony into every movie

Near the beginning of the
story, we know for sure
that these two characters
who can't stand each other
will kiss at the end
and be a couple AND
the characters don't
have a clue

From October
until the end of January,
the setting involves a
Christmas tree,
but besides that, Jenny
uses the formula
year around

Jenny was also enamored
with the words
ubiquitous
and
superfluous

I should have seen it coming

Sorry

Dear Southern Nevada

I noticed your walls first.
So many walls along the highway
and between neighborhoods
        sometimes with gates
and walls between neighbors

"Welcome to Las Vegas & Henderson,
Good luck meeting people"
it should say as you drive
in to town.

I noticed the rocks next.
Instead of grass,
I found more shapes, sizes,
and colors of rocks than I've
ever seen. Everywhere.
I am not a rock lover.

But I feel led here,
still feel I am in the right place.

So I turned to my new partner's friends
        one step forward
Began a job tutoring kids
        another step forward
Found an over 50 pick-up soccer community
        another step forward
Began attending the Unitarian Universalist congregation
        two giant steps forward ---

felt welcomed and valued
by fellow journeyers
(met a fellow poet...hi Stella!)
appreciated the pastor's
enthusiastic, joyful,
truth-telling ways.
And began to see that even
in this arid, isolating city
where people thirst secretly for community
where water is more sacred than church
I can
find ways to continue being
my active, service-minded, silly,
creative self
and
start to feel at home
again.

Until Then

My death will not be mentioned in the news

Neither for fame or infamy
I'd like to think

Until then
I will laugh
at Monty Python skits
of dead parrots
and men dressed as women

let my feet enjoy
Sade
Amy Winehouse
and
David Byrne

practice my faith
as I see fit
whether volunteering in the kitchen
at a camp for kids with cancer,
wishing everyone I come across
a good morning,
thinking before I speak,
hugging with conviction,
and giving with reckless abandon

Until
my-death-is-not-mentioned-in-the-news
I will play chess and
sing every chance I get

I will
notice Monarchs fluttering
notice my anger — and let it go —
notice the moment the orange sun rises
notice how your smile warms my heart

I will do my best
to notice

Overheard

This collection of words is not from my mouth. The words were overheard being spoken by my twenty-something friends working at Mackinac State Historic Park in the summer of 2022. I was a witness. "Fair enough" I hear them saying. I created the image at wordart.com

Spoiler Alert:
Politics and Justice

Bombarded

November, 2024

For years
I have been bombarded
by his negativity
and his arrogance

this Godless one
they see as a god

not once have I seen him
be kind unless he had
something to gain

over and over I have heard him
put down people of every kind
except his own breed

he wouldn't know a fact
if it slapped him in the face

he wouldn't know the truth
if it kicked him in the groin

this Godless one
they see as a god

as if God is a bully too

as if God is a bombardier
of negativity
and arrogance

Not my God

and now we will be
bombarded
for four more years —

God help us all

Responsibility Confronts Guilt

<table>
<tr><td valign="top">

R

You're not doing enough.

Jokes? You think now is the time for humor? These lunatics want to take the Movement back 30 years and you're making jokes?

t doesn't. You **are** pathetic but there's so much you could do if you'd get off your white, moderate butt and take some of me — take some responsibility — here you go. t's going to be risky and there are no guarantees but we have an obligation to **do** something.

</td><td valign="top">

G
I know, I know, I know. I'm racked with myself.

I'm not really feeling that funny. I'm feeling pathetic and impotent. And I feel bad about feeling pathetic and impotent, if that helps.

I don't deserve this. You've given me some of yourself. How unselfish of you. I don't think I can handle it. And I'll never be able to do enough. I never have before. Why do anything? I'm only one person; you're Mr. Responsibility, why don't **you** fix the world's problems?

</td></tr>
</table>

I'm already working overtime over here. Who do you think got President Joe to pardon all those people? Including Leonard Peltier and Marcus Garvey. We pushed through the cease-fire deal —

Sometimes we work together.

If I was in charge, Voting Day would be a day off for everyone and it would be a requirement, a law, that you have to vote.

My suggestion: work on yourself first. Be the guilt-free, progressive-acting change you want to see in the world.

Hold it. I thought I did the pardons.

Interesting. I do feel bad that so many of my friends chose not to vote.

Maybe I could help with that. Share some of myself with friends and Congressmen and women…give them the classic guilt trip from the master.

Yes, sir…right away, sir.

Almost Everything You Know is Wrong

it was the headline
this morning

the truest one lately

the world turns out
to be 10,000 times
more racist than I thought

and if I'm not part
of the answer
I'm part of the problem

>   what if my 7th grade self
>   had realized that?
>   how would my actions
>   have been different?

no one told me about
the Tulsa Massacre
or the extent and depravity
of lynchings

and what about in my
neighborhood? blatant
red-lining in   the   North

our country, it turns out,
doesn't welcome immigrants
with open arms anymore

I'm not asking for a
cheesy Utopia States of America

I would like to wake up
without fearing the headline

without doubting
my reality
and our future

Personally (from the POV of the USA)

I take all of these DOGE cuts very personally.

I am suddenly in a new relationship with a manipulative drama
queen and her domineering courtesan and they are giving me
a make-over against my wishes. They keep telling me it's for
my own good and for some reason, I'm going along with it.
This make-over involves deep liposuction to virtually every part
of my body. They jumped right in from day one of our
relationship nipping and tucking, slashing without cauterizing
— all without talking with me ahead of time.

Apparently, my gang of friends, with whom I usually consult
and constitutionally trust to be thinking of my best interests are
in on it too. All of them keep nodding and smiling like they've
drank so much Kool Aid that they are all hooked up to IVs of it.

None of them seem to be able or willing to see the long-term
effects on my body. First of all, I didn't think I was fat, in the
clinical sense. Sure, my stomach was pudgy but that kept me
(and you) warm in the winter. After the initial waves of surgery,
I am bruised in so many places that it hurts to move. My feet,
legs, arms, and hands hurt intensely — the pain is turning into
a numbness that I fear will end up causing nerve damage. And
how I feel — my mental, emotional, physical, spiritual
well-being matters to many others. People depend on me, and
now that I have been violated to this severe degree, I feel I will
be letting these people down.

I also fear infection from these numerous surgeries left open and exposed. I feel vulnerable. 250 years I have lived. But my future feels uncertain right now.

From

My Name is Aram, Too

A Hope Unspoken

Dedicated to my grandparents:
Mardiros (Baboo) and Kagazig Godoshian and Giragos
(Baboo) and Annig Kabodian

Sometimes I forget

they lived with the pain of their parents' murders
no safety net, no example, no peace
life was of their making
with a daily pain remembered

Sometimes I forget

they were so young and came so far
it could have been any place
but they settled here
led to this more perfect place

Sometimes I forget

they spoke from their hearts
but were not understood
for their words were foreign
this new land distrustful

Sometimes I forget

they coped with little
provided for many
complained minimally
praised the Lord

They laughed, sang, danced, hugged
life
with a hope unspoken:
my life.

Test Driving a Hearse

Our small town
Was growing too fast
For me
For its own good, forever
Unable to fit
Old, dark suits of expectation.

At first, though,
I didn't understand
Its growing pains.

And so, when Scott,
The friend my mom
Trusted completely
Asked
"Do you want to
Test drive a hearse?"
I was shocked.

We didn't do that stuff.
We were Bandos.
Went to catechism religiously.
Our gang were the
Altar boys,
Dutiful, proud, reverent.

"Really?" I questioned.
"Sure, it will be fun"

Was his quick response.
"I'll meet you there first thing,"
He said nonchalantly.

Early the next morning
I found myself
In the parking lot
Of Leadly Funeral Home.

Everyone had heard the stories
That Mr. Stone left the
Key to the hearse
Under the mat
On the driver's side.

I waited for Scott
Between the cars
And under a slight
Fog cover
For 15 minutes.

Eager to get it over with,
I checked the mat
For the key.

Found it with no problem
And sat in the driver's seat
Of the football-field long,
Cool, black death transfer unit.

Still no Scott.

Summoning my courage,
I turned it over,
And heard its soft purr.
Sliding the long arm
Down to Drive was
Easier than I thought
It would be.

Seeing up and over and out
The front windshield
Was more tricky.
I could barely reach
The gas pedal and see
Out at the same time.

I coasted quietly
Out of the lot
And down Main
As the sun thought about
Rising at the end of
First Street.

All "Go" lights at this hour
And no people around
Oddly enough.

As I reached the edge
Of town
I was starting to feel
Confident enough to push
The gas a bit harder.

Then I saw him.

Scott stood alone
In a parking lot
Under a new sign
That said "Hertz Car Rental."

Scott's mouth was open
As he walked over
To my window.

I cranked it down.
"You are in so much trouble"
He whispered.

All I could come up
With was
"You said hearse!"

From
People are Idiots

The Cemetery Loop

A peach sun glistens
on the trees
and on stone and gate
drawing me in
and I decide to include
the cemetery loop
on my evening walk.

Chupka's smiling face
is on his gravestone,
remembered as his
twenty-something bright-eyed self.

And Sweet left an
obelisk twice as high
as I am; it points
to the open sky
as if that's where we
could find Sweet if needed.

Someone decided to put
Law next to Jury
for comic effect
which I appreciated.

And I glimpse intense
tragedy in the stark

"Infant" alone on the stone.

Seeing the names of living friends
startles me.
I don't see my name
which is reassuring.
Though I did get mail once
addressed to
Kabochiak
and he is here
six feet below.

I feel oddly close
to these long gone strangers,
this graduation roll
to the Great Beyond.
I wonder how many of them
included the cemetery loop
in their evening walk
and
if any appreciated
my version of
May the Lord Bless Your Memory
and Keep You.

I hope.

Walking out of the gate
is its own blessing.

Reasons

I don't want to die:

They will get rid of my books

They won't understand
Assertive Black...Puzzled White
Takes me back forty years to that workshop
Reminds me how little I know

Furious Cool showed me a
Richard Pryor I had never known
Written by a boyhood acquaintance

In *Dreams in the Mirror*
I discovered e.e. cummings anew

They won't notice that Nikki Giovanni
Signed *ego-tripping* or be able to see
Her knowing smile from the plain cover

One Long River of Song will be just
Another collection of essays to sell
Instead of spiritual conversations
With a new friend

And I have the sense
I won't be able to be funny
Or laugh at a friend's joke

When I die

Or watch a glorious sunset
While I listen to my friend
Play taps on her French Horn
When I die

Steak and shrimp and shish kebob
Won't taste like anything
Sexandagoodcrapandadecentsleep
Won't be options

But the main reason
I don't want to die ---

They will get rid of my books

Appreciation

Yes, I wrote the poems. However, I live in a village that values the arts. And this village has helped put this book into your hands.

My main two readers have been Robin Boswell and Therese Dawe-Wood — both amazing writers themselves and both thankfully perceptive, honest, and gentle when sharing observations and opinions. I have also received encouraging feedback from Linda Ost, Delvar Dopson, Armen Kabodian, Teri Boling, Chance Liscomb, Troy Hicks, Sara Beauchamp-Hicks, Aaron Kabodian, my son, and Linda Jenkinson-Kabodian, my wife. Thank you one and all.

I want to especially thank Liz Stern for helping me to open my eyes, see the box I was in, and for emboldening me to conceive of a life outside the box. Her friendship goes back to moments like her recommendation that I might like James Taylor's *Gorilla* album. Life-changing then and now.

Julie Taylor (no relation that I'm aware of) from Michigan State University Libraries Publishing Service answered many questions about the publication process. Their website was also very practical and helpful. I continued learning at the Ingram Spark website which allowed the book to be available at bookstores.

Finally, I thank my parents, Zorob and Sally Kabodian for their love and support through the years. And for their reminders to be positive and find the humor in life.

Aram Kabodian's journey includes navigating Nevada, the joys of remarriage, working on Mackinac Island, volunteering, and watching sunrises.

His earlier poetry books can be found at aramkabodian.com or contacting Aram directly at akabodian@gmail.com